Letters to Myself

Volume 1
Self-harm & Suicide

By:
#1 International Bestselling Author
Jen Taylor, LCSW

ELITE PUBLISHING
HOUSE
YOUR LEGACY. YOUR BOOK.

First Edition

Copyright 2023 © Jen Taylor, LCSW

All Rights Reserved

No part of this book may be reproduced or transmitted in any form or by any means, electronic or mechanical, including photocopying, recording or by an information storage and retrieval system – except by a reviewer who may quote brief passages in a review to be printed in a magazine, newspaper or on the Web – without permission in writing from the publisher.

Photo Credits: Jen Taylor, LCSW
Cover Graphics: Kathryn Denhof

For my parents, Doctors Barbara & John Taylor, who taught me both the fragility and tenacity of living. And to Angel ...

UNITED STATES:

If you or someone you know is experiencing a mental health, suicide crisis, or emotional distress, reach out 24/7 to the 988 Suicide and Crisis Lifeline (formerly known as the National Suicide Prevention Lifeline) by dialing or texting <u>988</u> or using chat services at <u>suicidepreventionlifeline.org</u> to connect to a trained crisis counselor.

Please see Appendix Suicide Resources for Worldwide Numbers

TABLE OF CONTENTS

FOREWORD 7
   Ashok Gangadean, Ph.D.

INTRODUCTION 22

COLLECTION OF LETTERS 25
   Giancarlo Taylor Fani

   Blair Hayse

   Jessica Newell

   Gene Yonish

   Gene Yonish

   Gene Yonish

   M. LaRae, M. Sc.

   Marvin Ginsberg

   Lisa Powell

   Anonymous

MESSAGES OF HOPE 65

APPENDIX ON END - OF - LIFE CHOICES 68
   Includes 'Barbara's Choice' & Resources

APPENDIX ON SUICIDE RESOURCES 80

Includes Resources for Suicide Help & Assessment

CONDUCT A SUICIDE INQUIRY 95

DETERMINE RISK LEVEL 98

ABOUT THE AUTHOR 100

FOREWORD

Prologue on the Root Causes of Suicide©
Ashok Gangadean, Ph.D.
Professor of Global Philosophy
Haverford College

Understanding the Depth Origins of Suicide

The issue of "suicide" runs deep and has been of primary importance to First Philosophers and Enlightened Teachers through the ages on a planetary scale. The Life and Death issues surrounding "suicide" are not only psychological concerns and symptoms of "mental health" (important as these are) but also existential and ontological (Science of Being), touching into the very depth of what it means to Be, gaining access to the very Source of Life, the Meaning of Life, the Nature of the Self, to Be or not to Be, our perennial quest for Happiness, Personal Fulfilment, Self-Worth and Well Being. When our Lives flow in the voltage of Meaning and Value the Lights are On and we flourish, but when we are alienated from the Source of Life and the Light of Being we can fall into a certain existential darkness, despair, nihility and depression

(Lights dimmed or out), with no authentic *Raison d'Être* and no *Joie de Vivre*.

The traditions of First Philosophy focus with Medical urgency on the need of us Humans to focus with utter priority on **What is First** (by whatever Name), on Being, Primary Reality, the Source of all Existence, the Origin of Meaning, Value and Truth.

Socrates, for example, in the Classical Greek "Logos" tradition suggests that everyday Humans are as if "living in a cave of Ignorance" and urgently need to enter the Philosophical enterprise of leaving the cave of shadows and cross into the Light of Logos, the call to Know thy true Self. The Philosophical Life for Socrates is the preparation (through the Rational Enterprise) for a true Death that releases our Primary Self (Soul) into the enlightened Wisdom of Logos.

Buddha's enlightenment, too, was an onto-medical breakthrough to the source of human existential suffering in its many forms. Buddha found that Human suffering is caused by chronic addiction to deeply entrenched mental processes that objectify the Self and alienates us from direct access to authentic Life in touch with Reality. Buddha's ontological medicine called for a radical and systemic rehabilitation of our "mentation process" that breaks the addictive trance of predominant "ego mental practices" in Self making, World making, culture and experience processing. This rehabilitation of our culture making "technology" is the key to ending wide ranging existential suffering and for our advance to human flourishing and well-being.

So, too, with the Life Coaching of Lord Krishna in the classical *Bhavagad-gita*. Krishna coaches Arjuna, the Warrior-leader of his army (a stand in for everyday Humans) as he suffers an existential melt-down on the battle-field amidst an agonizing fratricidal war. Arjuna's life-world falls apart in a Life Crisis as his higher conscience cautions him against a "justified war" wherein he has to kill members of his Family for rightful Kingship. Arjuna, in deep despair, drops his weapon, melts down, and turns to Lord Krishna (Avatar of AUM, the Field of Being) for onto-medical assistance and moral guidance.

Here, again, in this First Teaching, Krishna introduces Arjuna to the Technology of Yoga, the heart of Vedic (Meditative) Science which focuses on the evolutionary rite of passage from the obsolete and dysfunctional mentation processes that privilege the ego-mental stage of human development to a more evolved technology of Life-making that generates the Integral and Holistic Self-making and Life-production that brings the end of Samsaric suffering and lifts all Humans to Self-Liberation and Flourishing in communion with Being.

In this 2,500-year scan of First Teachers in a Global Light we find an analogous Life coaching in our Judeo-Christian Biblical tradition in the First Teachings of Jesus. From an Ontological point of view this tradition, too, notices that when we humans are alienated from our Primary Source of Life (the existential condition of "Sin") we face a Life and Death issue and it will take a radical onto-medical rite of passage to overcome this existential alienation and rise to true Meaning and Well Being in a higher form of life. Jesus (in the Office of Christ, Logos in the flesh), speaks and embodies the Logos Code in his Life Coaching suggesting that in some sense we must "Die" to be "Born Again". This rite of passage from alienated life to Communion with Being, the essence of First Teachings, calls for a detachment or letting go of self-privileged Narratives of Life and Self to Honor Logos (Infinite Presence) as First.

Of course, this theme of the Primordial and Perennial Human Quest for Primary Being, for Well-being and Flourishing, resonates through the Centuries in our diverse First Teachings and haunts the evolutionary development of our European cultural journey. From Descartes' *Meditations on First Philosophy* and beyond into the innovations of Husserl, Heidegger and Sartre (Existentialism) and others we find the relentless quest for our true and authentic Self in the Existentialist turn in First Philosophy. And it is in this context that we find, for example, the voice of existential author Albert Camus:

There is but one truly serious philosophical problem, and that is suicide. Judging whether life is or is not worth living amounts to answering the fundamental question of philosophy.

Albert Camus: The Myth of Sisyphus

The Ontology of "Suicide" in a Global Light

It makes all the difference to situate the realities of "suicide" in the foundational context of the **Science of Being (Ontology)** since, as we shall now see, the Life and Death issues of "suicide" turn essentially on chronic alienation from primary access to Being. The Psychology of Suicide is a derivative narrative space from The Ontology of Suicide: and **Medical Ontology (A Foundational Science)** reveals how and why forms of life alienated from and severed from access to Primary Being suffer wide ranging existential pathologies of life.

In this Global Light we are able to see more clearly that diverse forms of "suicide" are not in a "silo" but are more localized onto-medical symptoms of wide-ranging Human Dysfunctions of Ill-Being. If our Being is ill (a life in the eclipse of Being) we Humans suffer existential ailments of widely diverse forms, and the mentation virus of "suicide" is one onto-medical effect of the generic alienation from Being (Reality). This depth Diagnostic of the roots of "Suicide" is essential in effectively healing our broken worlds and chronically fragmented lives.

It is clear that Suicide (and "Suicidal Ideation") remain an ever-growing cultural epidemic in our contemporary Human Condition. And given the global consensus of our First Teachings - calling for all Persons to come face to face with how we are making our Selves and our Worlds and to have the courage to face the ground floor of Reality, the Foundation of Being, the Primary Source of Life and Human Existence- it remains stunning that our Human Family has NOT yet truly processed this. Why have we (apparently) not yet tapped more effectively the enormous Medical Resource of our collective Wisdom and Enlightenment teachings?

We ARE as we Mind

When we remain chronically alienated from direct access to our Primary Being, to the Source of Life, Meaning and Value we suffer existential pathologies. **We ARE as we "mind"**: the presiding "mentation code" operative in co-shaping our Self, our Experience, our World, our Life makes all the difference to our Quality of Life. If our mind operating "software" is compromised, dysfunctional in any way, encodes an **existential virus**, we will suffer existential disorders at the personal and cultural levels. **Let's call this the "Mentation" process**. In this context we see that "Mental Health" requires **Mentation Health**, Competence and Literacy.

In the Medical Ontology of our First Teachings, we humans have been deeply entrenched in **mind operating processes** that inherently eclipse direct access to Source Life and alienate us from our healthful Primary Form of Life. The **Meaning of Life** is not merely linguistic or logical or conventional, but is Life Itself. A **Meaningful Life is Existential**, is a Mindful Life, and our diverse First Teachers have been calling us with highest urgency to upgrade our Mentation Processing. But we have not yet introduced effective **((Mentation Code Markers))** to bring to open clarity which mind operating ((code)) in fact is implicitly and silently presiding in shaping our Lives and our Mentation Health.

If our presiding mind operating code (logic or consciousness technology) is pathologically derivative from Primary Being, and without our knowledge or consent fragmenting our life, psyche, self, experience and mental health then this medical condition generates deep existential pathologies of life. And this is where we find the origins of serious Life and Death pathologies such as suicide, human violence and ill-Being.

But if we are able to self-transform our Mentation Code to the prescriptions of First Science then we cross into a more healthful personal and cultural space that overcomes widespread existential pathologies (including suicidal disorders) and brings foundational Well Being and Personal and Cultural flourishing.

The state of our "Mental Health" and Existential Health are directly related to the Competence and Integrity of our Mentation Process. We are as we "code": and if our dominant mind-code fragments, polarizes and atomizes all it touches then our lived experience, our psychological states, our quality of Life will reflect existential ailments and wide-ranging pathologies. This is the Medial context in which various forms of "suicide" are to be situated, understood and treated. This is the deep diagnosis of Medical First Teachings.

Facing the "Mentation" Issue: Our Mind-operating ((Codes))

But without clear and explicit **((mentation code markers))** our Human Family remains lodged in a certain deep and chronic Mentation Code Chaos when our existential alternative **Life Codes** are perpetually conflated. In the Light of Global First Philosophy and Source Science it is clear that without the differentiating power of explicit Life Code Markers our Human Family has been making our Selves and our Lives in the **Age of Life Code Conflation**.

This failure to become keenly aware of which Life Code we are laboring under and presiding in the existential quality of our lives is a primary Onto-Medical Cause of our individual and collective failure to openly access the enormous Life Transforming Medical Resources of our First Teachings. We Humans have been living and operating within the Code

Chaos and ambiguous Code Conflation Syndrome for centuries, and this has contributed to our being rather stalled and hitting an invisible pathological Life Code ceiling and barrier that blocks our healthful and open access to ((Source Life)).

In the rather limited time and space of this compressed Prologue it is not appropriate to get into the introduction of the Life Code markers that I found necessary to introduce some decades ago. The contrasting ((code markers)) has been developed in great depth in other contexts. In brief, on this occasion, I'll only stipulate that I introduced **Existential Life Code markers: "/…/" and "((…))"**
to de-conflate and make explicit the contrasting Life Codes that are all important to our First Teachings.

Once we end the Code chaos and dysfunctional Code conflation a profound and dramatic transformation takes place: we are able to see clearly that our First Teachers were calling us to **shift from /life processing/ to ((Life Processing))**. They were each calling for a deep existential shift from a derivative /mentation process/ to a more healthful and primary ((Life Code)). When we live and operate within Code Chaos we invariable default to the more adolescent and secondary /Life Code/ that is inherently lodged in fragmentation, polarization. Objectification of Self and Other, which generates existential fragmentation, isolation, patterns of violence, and the eclipse of ((Being)) ((Life)) ((Self)) and ((Meaning)). But if we are not facing the Code Mentation issue, and not even aware that there is a ((Life Code)) shift, how is it possible to competently and effectively make the existential ((shift)) from /Life/ to ((Source Life))?

In this ((Global Light)) of ((Source Science)) and Life Code Literacy we are empowered with a deeper ((Agency)) to ((Mind)) our /Minding/ as never before and break through the invisible /code barriers/ and tap the Potent Medicine of our First Teachers: we can ((see)) and ((make the shift)) from /Life/ to ((Source Life)). And this is the Medical Ontology that gets to the heart of various forms of Suicide and "Suicide Ideation". Pathological "Ideation" flourishes in cultural spaces of Mentation Chaos and Mentation dysfunction.

I realize that this ((Prologue)) on the Origins of Suicidal Pathologies is just an opening ((Introduction)). And I hope and trust that the foregoing will bring new Onto-Medical Hope for deep healing of our Selves, our Lives and our Cultures.

I offer this ((Prologue)) in support of the publication of my Friend and former Student, Jen Taylor:

Letters to myself Volume I: self-harm and suicide
Jen Taylor LCWS
Elite Publishing

Jen brings together in this volume powerful and moving personal narratives of courageous individuals who have faced and struggled with issues of existential suicide and suicidal ideation. I hope my foregoing ((Prologue)) helps set a meaningful ((context)) to appreciate the heart-felt voices in these letters.

I also offer the following ((Ode to Life)) Parts I and II to further deepen this ((Prologue Reflection))

Ashok Gangadean
Margaret Gest Professor of Global Philosophy
Haverford College
October 18, 2023

((Ode to Life))©
Ashok Gangadean
March 26, 2023

Part I

((Welcome to Presence
Alas this is Home
LogosSophia's communion
God, Christ and AUM

Portal to Presence Heavenly Doors
Always inviting ever open to Knowers

Being ever Flowing in Stillness of NOW
Peace and Love Blissing, never mind How

Heavenly Music Sacred the Sound
Harmony Flowing Nirvana Un bound

Life in Elation Love Everywhere
Sophia's New Nation no more Despair

Logos Creation Life in Light Flows
First Persons of Fire Whole Cosmos Glows

Hatred and Strife Now disappears
Despair and Negation End of All Fears

Nature Smiling All Creatures give Shout
Joyous Celebration Rapture Sings Out

Eros Joins Reason End of the Chasm
Earth Couples with Heaven in Life's Orgasm

Fragrance of Presence Heavenly Sent
Earth Angels Dancing in Joyous Ascent

Earth rests in Heaven Unum Abounds
Symphonic Attunement Freedom Resounds

Welcome to Presence This is the Way
Make Your Self Comfortable
Do Hope We'll Stay))

Part II

(((/How can I enter
Have I the right?

I'm living in Sin
Haven't earned yet the rite/))

((All Humans are Coded
Grace gifted to Zone

Once you have entered
You're never A-lone

((I- Thou)) is Flowing
Put away your I-Phone

Mindfulness is your Pass Word
((I am)) is your ((code))

When you detach from your /Past/
Your true Self Awakens

It may feel like a dying
But is Re-Birth in the Making

This code crossing is scarry
Do I dare ((enter))?

Be Still, take a Breath
You're already at Center

When you code cross to Presence
Your true ((life)) commences

Welcome to Presence
Put away all defenses))

Ashok Gangadean
Margaret Gest Professor of Global Philosophy, Haverford College
Director, Margaret Gest Center for Dialogue Beyond Borders
Founder-Director of the ((Global Dialogue Institute))
www.awakeningmind.org
email: agangade@haverford.edu

INTRODUCTION

You may be wondering what prompted me to create a book on this topic.

Two things:

Firstly, I have always been that person who brings up the hard-to-talk-about stuff. Even as a child and teenager, I remember telling my dad, *"I don't want to talk about B.S. like the weather. I want to talk about important things."* Needless to say, he was not pleased with my use of language, but he got the gist of what I was saying.

Astrologically, individuals born in the mid-1960s, 1965 to 1967, have a conjunction of Uranus and Pluto. These are people around the age of 56/57/58 today. We are truth-seekers who do not play by the ordinary rules of society. The closer the conjunction is, the more this is true. We may be considered the "rebels" in society. There is usually a cause for our rebellion. In my life, I have often brought up the complex topics, things people want to hide or sweep under the rug. It can be uncomfortable and sometimes painful, but, in the end, truth is the victor and helps us to heal.

A couple of years ago, toward the end of COVID-19, I brought my teenage daughter to see a doctor at NYU Langone in NYC. I was given a sheet of paper that stated the staff might speak with my daughter about mental health. The flyer said that suicide was the #2 cause of death among adolescents in the U.S. I was shocked and deeply saddened by this statistic. After much thought and discussion with family, friends, and colleagues, I decided to gather a collection of letters on suicide and self-harm. It was my great hope that sharing our own painful experiences and how we were able to overcome them might offer an alternative to a young person contemplating suicide. I believe that if someone is hell-bent on committing, there is nothing we can do to dissuade them.

On the other hand, attempts and self-harm are often a cry for help. Many suicide attempts fail because the individual may not have been 100% sure of their decision and because many methods are not foolproof. If there is even a 1% chance that the individual wants to live, let's grab that and run with it!!

Many thanks to the brave authors who have shared their harrowing stories anonymously and named Marvin Ginsberg, Giancarlo Taylor Fani, Blair Hayse, M. LaRae, M. Sc., Jessica Newell, Lisa Powell & Gene Yonish.

Heartfelt thanks to my spiritual teacher, Elizabeth Myers, without whom I would not be in this place today!! *"Life is for living!"* And to my children, for reflecting back the deepest love I feel for them in my saddest moments and reminding me that I am a good mom.

Thank you to Blair Hayse, Elite Publishing House, Kathryn Denhof (graphics), and my professor and mentor, Prof. Ashok Gangadean for breathing life into this concept.

Thank you for purchasing this book so that we can spread hope together. 25% of proceeds will be donated to The Trevor Project, an agency that helps at-risk youth in the suicide prevention efforts in the LGBTQIA+ community.

As the Italians say, *"La speranza e' l'ultima a morire."* (Hope is the last to die).

I have also included a list of hotlines and resources to help in our battle against suicide.

COLLECTION OF LETTERS

It's been over two years since I tossed my life in the air like a coin flip. There was no question of regret or consequence that night. When I look back on this night, there are nothing but thoughts of the consequences of what could have been my last decision. When in that space, none of the aftermath matters. All that matters is making the pain stop and ensuring the hypothetical future pain doesn't have the chance to add to it. At the time, I had a girlfriend who would have done anything to see me happy, many good friends who never let me feel alone, and a family who made sure I was always unconditionally loved. From an outside perspective, I had an amazing life.

A life I took for granted. Although I was laughing all the time and mostly always had good company, I was numb and really depressed. At the same time, I preferred isolation. Taking a pill or buying some drinks and playing games was much more enticing to me than spending the day with my girlfriend or seeing my best friend, whom I secretly wished I could be with at the time. I was consumed by addiction and instant gratification. Without being able to appreciate the things I had; I could only think of how much better it could be. When someone does decide to take their life, it usually doesn't matter if you have a lot of love or support. It is the perspective that makes you have tunnel vision. That being said, that perspective can change. Making that decision at that moment could have been the end. For a lot of people who do decide to attempt, it sadly is the end. There usually isn't thought that there can be a shift in perspective. It often feels too hopeless to see that if you are suicidal.

For me, thankfully, that perspective did end up changing. A little over two years later, I can't even see a world where I would give up the potential of the future. Forgiving the past you is essential in healing and moving on to a positive future. On that night, I took a mixture of two types of pills, Ambien and Xanax, as well as a generous amount of wine, probably more than a 750 ml bottle. The mix of the medications alone should have killed me. The alcohol mixed with either one alone can also lead to fatal results. I proceeded to go to bed, crying and thinking of all my loved ones.

Although I didn't care enough to spare them the pain of losing me, I did send a message to a few people thanking them for the love they gave and apologizing for the pain it would cause (as if that would do anything). I honestly didn't think anyone would care at the time. I did include "in case I don't wake up" before saying thanks and sorry. I didn't quite know how likely waking up would be, but the chances were slim considering how much I consumed, with all the interactions, etc., there was almost no way. My faith in God is "streaky" per se. If there is a God or some higher power, I believe that night, they spared me and those who care for me from a dark fate. Whether it was God or just some miracle, I woke up the next day… And I cannot describe in words how fucking grateful I am for still being here. Not thinking people cared, I was also overwhelmed with how many people actually did care. I felt so bad for worrying them, but seeing how much my presence on earth impacted them was very emotional. The things I have learned and experienced since then, in just a short amount of time, already made still being alive worth it. The things I have felt and the relationships I have made/strengthened since then have been magical. I love being alive. The world needs me. Even if that is just for those few people I impact or for many, many more than I expect to impact in the future, it is all worth it.

If you can get anything from reading this, please make it this.

STAY, Tomorrow needs you.

It will get better, no matter how much you think it won't.

Love your life, and never give up on yourself.

- Giancarlo Taylor Fani

To The One Who Tried to End It -

Oh, dear friend. I am sure that there was a day you looked in the mirror and never thought you would reach the end. You thought you would always find that one reason to get up each morning. Maybe it was work, your children, your marriage, or perhaps the mere fact that you feared death too much.

Sure, you had your down days. You had the days that you purely melted down. Maybe you broke down and cried in the shower, letting the water wash over you and wishing it would wash away all the pain you felt deep inside. Maybe you went to bed at night and took sleeping pills, hoping you wouldn't wake up in the morning. Then, when you did, you weren't sure if you were relieved or not. Maybe you came home to an empty home and picked up a dish, smashed it in pieces, then sank to the floor in a mess of tears and fell asleep on the floor. Maybe you cut yourself off from friends and hobbies. You secluded yourself. You never opened your blinds and never wanted to see the sun. Perhaps you preferred to sleep instead of be awake. Maybe it was all too easy to pour another glass of vodka and down another pain pill to keep the hurt away.

Slowly, the bad days outnumbered the good days. Your friends withered away. They didn't notice that you were not around much, and then you realized they wouldn't notice if you were gone altogether. Suddenly, you started to realize there was no reason for you to stay around. You occupied your time piecing together why you should stay, and there weren't many reasons on the list. Soon, you justified those away. Soon, you carefully put together your perfect plan of how you wanted things to be once you were gone. I mean, someday you were going to die. That is something that does happen to everyone. You wrote notes to those you cared about and picked out your outfit, perhaps. You tied up loose ends. You carefully texted those friends you never talked to anymore to tell them goodbye in a somewhat carefree way, and with the way they had disappeared from your life, they never thought twice about that text.

Then, one day, you woke up. It was a bad day. You probably didn't even want to get out of bed. All those reasons you always gave yourself for living life seemed very distant. Maybe you poured another drink sooner in the day than usual, maybe you called into work, perhaps you made an excuse to stay home or in your room, and all the pain seemed heavier than normal. Then, you did what you never thought you would do. You decided life was better with you gone. You didn't fear death anymore because you finally saw relief in it. You saw no more pain. You saw that something had to be better than the way you kept living. You knew everyone would be okay without you, probably much better off without you. You didn't worry about it anymore. You wanted to find peace and a sweet release from the hurt. You pulled the trigger, you downed the pills, you took your life into your own hands.

The next few moments were probably a shadowy mix of subconscious memories. What seemed like just moments was an eternity. Probably people banging on doors, shaking you, begging you to talk, or trying to figure out how far gone you were. Police and ambulance workers. Some you remember—some you don't. People say, *"Don't leave me, hang on."* Then things go black. Days are lost until you gain your memory back. Then you wondered if you were happy you were here or sad you didn't leave. You brushed the side of death. People probably were in disbelief that you did it and never saw it coming, even though you thought, how could they have missed it for the years you felt it coming?

You have obviously recovered if you are reading this. You probably went through rehab. You gained your life back. Now, life has more good days than bad. You pull the curtains back and enjoy the sunshine. Some days, you still have a bad day, and some days, you still feel pain. Some days, you actually scare yourself by wondering if you could ever slip that far again because you never thought you could before. You never judge others anymore because you know how it feels.

Somewhere deep in your heart, the pain still sits. And somewhere deep in your heart, you still have days you ask yourself if you should have died that day. Yes, you do still wonder if you should be here. You have moments of weakness; they are just very few. It is okay. We are overcomers. We are the weak that were made strong. We not only saw death, felt death, but lived death. We have a right to be weak every once in a while. We wonder how we got there because we never thought we could be weak. It is in those moments of weakness we find our strength.

Stay strong, my dear friend.

- Blair Hayse

I had always been told that everyone's story matters. I never really believed that, mainly because I don't think I fully understood what it meant. What does it mean to matter, to matter truly? I always thought it meant something had to have a certain level of importance. My story had to make sense. It had to resonate with everyone. My story couldn't be ugly or unsettling. It needed to be presented in a pretty manner and wrapped up in a perfect package with a neat bow on the top. So, what if none of that applies to me? What if my story doesn't meet those requirements? Does that mean it doesn't matter, that I don't matter?

The truth is that there is no perfect way to tell a story, especially about personal things. You may not think that it matters. It's just something that happened to you, it's just a struggle you've gone through, it's just a part of your past. It's so much more than that. It's a part of who you are, but that doesn't mean it has to define your future or how you see yourself. I've always wondered if talking about what I've gone through would make a difference. Would it matter? I'll let you decide for yourself.

I grew up in a very religious family that taught me to respect others, to be kind, and to always put others before yourself. I took those values to heart. I was always nice to everyone I met, I made sure to stay respectful, and I never put myself first, no matter what the situation was. I allowed people to push me around, and I never thought twice about it because that was how I was raised. I was never really taught that I could say no. I was never told I could set boundaries. So, I let people cross lines. I allowed them to treat me however they wanted because I didn't know any different. I was told by several people growing up that depression and anxiety were just things you could pray away. Just stop worrying so much, stop being emotional, try to be more active, try not to let things get to you. It was just something you went through, and it wasn't anything to be concerned about.

I remember in fifth grade; there was a group of girls in the grade above me who used to tease me. They'd boss me around and make me feel like garbage if I disobeyed. I was very young at the time, so it never crossed my mind that they were bullying me. I always assumed it was because they were older, and I always respected and did what my elders told me to do. When you're a kid, you never really expect to be treated harshly, so when it happens, you don't recognize it as bad behavior at first. When I started seventh grade, my school, Colbert County High School, welcomed students from another school, Hatton Elementary, because that school didn't have a high school for the students to attend. It wasn't new; they had always done this, but thinking about all the new friends I might make was exciting. It, however, did not work out that way. I didn't know these kids; I didn't grow up with them, and they didn't know me. I was quiet, I kept to myself, I was a bigger girl, I had glasses, I was your typical bullied kid stereotype. It all began with one of the transfer students from the other school.

Looking back at it now, it almost felt like she made it her job to make me feel like nothing. From seventh grade to ninth grade, to bullied me relentlessly. She would call me horrible names, she made jokes about my weight and my appearance, she made comments about my hygiene, etc. Eventually, it wasn't just her alone. Other students joined in on the "fun." A group of boys would say things about my weight, and they would make obscene comments about me and my body. Most of the time, the bullying's focal point was my weight. It got so bad to the point where I wouldn't eat lunch some days because I feared what they would say to me.

It even became physical when a cheerleader, who had a locker above me in my ninth-grade year, would drop her textbooks and notebooks on my head anytime we were at the lockers together. During class, I would have pencils, pens, highlighters, etc., thrown at me as I sat at my desk. I was pushed while in the hallways and walking up and down the stairs. I was terrified, constantly, of just how physical it was going to get. I never wanted to be alone due to the fear of possibly being randomly attacked or hurt.

As a teenager, it's easy to let things get to you. You're immature and naïve; most of the time, you'll believe almost anything. The "jokes" that were made about my physical appearance affected me the most. At first, I tried to brush it off and told myself not to think about what they were saying. It just kept getting worse and harder for me to shut them out.

Eventually, I let their words sink in. I let them take over. I allowed them to control how I viewed myself. I chose what I wore to school based on what I thought they might say. I styled my hair a certain way. I made sure to wear particular shoes. I let it dictate every aspect of my life.

In eighth grade, I stopped eating. I thought maybe things would be better if I looked more like the girls teasing me. I wanted to fit in so badly. I just wanted the ridicule and torment to stop. I wanted them to see me as a friend and not a mistake. So, I skipped meals when I could. I ate just enough in front of my friends and family to not raise suspicion, only allowing myself small amounts even then. I made sure to weigh myself as often as possible. I wanted to be perfect so that they would like me. It didn't matter how dizzy I felt, how my vision would blur from time to time, how my head would throb in the middle of class. I shoved all that aside. I pushed through my body's agony because all that mattered was being good enough for my tormentors. Suppose I ate more than I was supposed to; if I had too many soft drinks or ate a piece of candy, I would punish myself. I wanted to feel something, anything. So, I began to cut my arms, legs, stomach, and anywhere I didn't like on my body. I used razors, box cutters, and anything sharp that would pierce through the skin everyone hated so much. Choosing not to eat and letting the blood drip from my veins was the only thing I felt I had control over in my life.

Have you ever had something or someone completely alter who you are? Did you choose to make those changes, or did it seem like you had to? Did your insecurities and emotions make the decision for you? Did you accept your fate because that seemed like the only thing left to do? The things we say and do always have a side effect. You never really know how long you can take the pain until something pushes you over the edge. One word, one action, can drive someone to the breaking point.

My breaking point happened on October 12, 2013. It was a Saturday, which meant no school, so I was safe. At least, I thought I was. I was alone at home; my parents were running errands, and I decided not to join them. I was watching TV when I got a text notification on my phone. I picked up thinking it was one of my parents, siblings, or even one of my few friends. The last thing I expected was a text from an unknown number. The messages kept coming through, one right after the other.

Ding! *"You're such a loser."*
Ding! *"Nobody wants you around."*
Ding! *"Do you actually think your friends like you?"*
Ding! *"You're disgusting."*
Ding! *"No one would miss you."*
Ding! *"DISAPPEAR!"*

With each message, my vision began to blur, and I could feel my heart pounding in my chest. The room seemed to get smaller, and every sound around me seemed to fade in and out. Looking back now, I understand that I was not in control of myself or my emotions. I had given up. I had stopped fighting the voice in my head telling me to keep going and keep trying. The words in those messages were on replay in my mind. Maybe they were right. Maybe things would be better if I just…. disappeared. I wouldn't have to worry about school anymore. I wouldn't have to deal with the verbal and physical assaults. The anger and frustration, the pain, the sadness, all of that would disappear if I did. I wouldn't be a burden to anyone anymore.

I ran to the bathroom and grabbed a bottle of pills that had my name on it. The pills were muscle relaxers, which meant they were supposed to help with your pain. I took every pill that was left in that bottle. I just wanted to stop the pain; I wanted it to disappear, and if, in the process, I disappeared, then that was just a bonus. I remember bits and pieces of what happened after. I remember my parents coming home. I remember us going out to eat, me being disgusted by the smell of food, and vomiting in the restaurant bathroom after having a few bites of food. I remember walking out of the restaurant and my legs feeling numb. I remember grabbing my mom's arm and crying. I remember being in the emergency room, hearing muffled cries of my mother asking for help, and being put in a wheelchair. That's where it fades out. It all went black.

When I woke up, my mother was standing beside my hospital bed, my dad sitting in a chair to the left of me. I looked over to my mom, and she immediately called a nurse to come in. They checked my vitals and began asking me all sorts of questions. My mother kept asking me why I did it, how I could make such a choice, and why I would do this to her and my dad. I didn't want to answer, mainly because I knew she wouldn't like what I would say. A part of me wanted to keep my mouth shut, not talk about the reason, not tell her how much pain I was in. I thought it would just make things worse; it wouldn't help anyway, so why bother her or anyone else with my issues? My mouth moved a lot faster than my brain did, and I just said, *"I couldn't do it anymore,"* and I started to cry.

"Couldn't do what?" she asked me. Live, I thought. I couldn't bring myself to say it out loud. So, I just stared at the ceiling and cried. I was angry. Angry that I was still here, angry that the pills didn't do what they said they would, angry that the doctors had saved me. It took me six years to stop being angry. I'm still working on trying to be thankful and understand that there was a reason why my life didn't end that day. I'm here for a reason...a purpose, even if I'm unsure what it is.

- Jessica Newell

Suicide.
I believed the many lies,
About myself.
I took the bottles of pills off the shelf.
Many tears.
Endless fears.
My deaf ears.
The bottle got more and more near.
"What do I do?"
Happy days so few.
My only relief was in the church pew.
"I want to pray?
What do I say,
To the Almighty One,
Reached by way of God's Son?"
Heaven won.
2023.
I'm alive.
I've been set free.
Give me a high five.
Let's celebrate.
It ain't too late.
Wait.
Is it really me?
Let's see.
No more insanity.
You would definitely agree.
Praises to God!
No longer am I odd.

I'd love to tell you more.
Let's get together over scones and tea.
Your feelings will soar,
Too.
I grew.
You can, too.

- Gene Yonish

I, Gene, have a history of suicidal experiences. I tried to do myself in on three specific occasions, with overdoses of pills. I was extremely depressed and wasn't that verbal when I was younger. My suicide attempts were in 1983, 1987, and 1992. I was suffering inside and didn't feel comfortable talking to anyone about it. I isolated myself a lot. I also wasn't that engaged with my Christian faith at the time. And I had no work life. I would wake up and immediately start sobbing for a while, and this happened for extended periods of time.

- Gene Yonish

Dear Gene,

"You've come a long way, baby!" I remember how much stress you caused us during your inpatient hospitalization at both Nassau County Medical Center and Columbia Presbyterian Medical Center. You really weren't a very nice person back then. The crazy phone calls. The harassing phone calls. Your incoherent speech. We called you every day at one point to make sure that you were alive. How you worried us, especially with regards to the days before you were hospitalized, being that you were involuntarily hospitalized. Gene, you were declared a missing person. That's pretty serious. Gene, you sure had lots of energy for a very sick person. When you retold us what exactly happened, where you hid yourself, etc., wow!! You were like a professional escape artist. Where did you get all that energy to walk from Glen Cove to Jericho? Gene, you did make one glaring mistake. When you called Steve to meet you at Sun Up Pizza, you told him you were worried about Audrey. As you later found out, Steve called us. Uncle Yogi really cared and cared about you. Of course, you found out that it was a setup. And we had to get the police involved. We suspected you weren't taking your medication and needed to be kept safe and hospitalized. After all, we didn't know what kind of shape that we'd find you in. You sure are full of drama.

- Gene Yonish

At the time, I don't know what was more disappointing, the fact that I felt the urge to attempt or that I woke up the next morning. That was the reality of my emotional state in my early 20s.

I lived at a low-income trailer park without a vehicle and what felt like without a soul in the world to confide in, share with, or spend time with. I felt utterly alone. Mind you, this trailer was barely holding itself together, with pieces of the floor missing, and I felt that pieces of myself were also missing. So, the trailer and I were both feeling broken down and barely holding it together.

How did I get here? Growing up, I wasn't born into wealth or riches, but we usually had a houseful of friends and family to share our daily experiences with. So where did I end up feeling so very alone?

From birth to early pre-teen, we lived in a rural farming community. My grandparents were farmers, and most of the family, including all of us kids, worked in the fields. During the summer, when school was out, we were in the fields gathering vegetables from early morning until everything was finished for the day. That often meant late nights with siblings, cousins, aunts, grandparents, and other workers. In other words, I was not isolated in any sense of the word. My daily experiences were almost always filled with family and friends.

Yet here I was in my early 20s, feeling like life had nothing to offer.

But still, how did I end up here, alone, to the point of not wanting to continue breathing air? At the time, I was in the middle of experiencing a violent and abusive relationship. During the moments that I attempted to no longer spend my days breathing, our relationship was in the off position. Unfortunately, that would crank back up soon enough. I know this not because of my attempt but because I told nobody until over 30 years later that it happened. If I could reach back and talk to that young woman to reassure her that everything will be okay and things do get better, would she have heard me? Would she have the strength to trust what I'm saying? Could she, at that point, believe me?

These are answers that I will never know.

I remember thinking about the combination of pills and alcohol and wondering if I could take enough, then could I rest. That was a long time before Google, so I didn't do any research on how much it might take. It seems like word of mouth and probably television had instilled a thought of the lethal combination. I vaguely remember my mom attempting it when I was a child, and that was through an overdose of pills. So, I guess somehow that seemed plausible. And coupled with some alcohol, how could I fail?

I remember just sitting on my couch and thinking about whether I could go ahead and take my concoction of pain relief. That's how I felt about this decision. I don't believe that I wanted to stop breathing at all. I was instead exhausted in every way possible. I was tired of trying...look where that had taken me. I was tired of thinking about what I hadn't done and the ways that I felt I had failed. I was tired of feeling alone. I was just tired and could not see past where I was at that moment. There was no internet, cell phones, or social media available, just me and the silence.

I cried for a little bit after I swallowed them. I knew I couldn't turn back now. So, I curled up in the corner of my couch and waited to rest. Though a bit groggy, my body was conditioned to wake up in time for work, and without fail, my body woke me up in time to get ready for the daily grind. Luckily, one of my co-workers came by as planned to pick me up, and I just went about my business, but now with another feeling of failure.

Not knowing until later in life that I had unresolved childhood trauma, I felt as though I had to deal with everything on my own. I felt like no one could or would help me. From childhood, I had internally decided to deal with everything alone. Not knowing this at the time just left me feeling alone and hurting with nowhere I thought I could turn. These feelings were temporary; however, I couldn't see past them at that moment.

Life has turned so far around, and beautiful experiences have filled my world in ways I literally could not have imagined. I've studied the energy field and learned how I can direct my life intentionally and that I do choose my experiences. That has given me strength and direction that I didn't know existed.

I'm glad that I didn't know the right amount to take. I'm glad that my body apparently rejected what I tried to force. I don't know if someone could've helped me in those moments, but I do know that I didn't give anyone the chance.

I fully believe that many people decide this path with full cognition and acceptance for many different reasons, and that is their choice. For others, like myself, it was a try to stop the pain attempt that, fortunately for me, I did fail.

If anyone feels the need to talk about where they are and where they can go in life, there are many people who are willing to listen and help. Just reach out. Give someone the chance to help. Sometimes, I think people need someone to listen. Sometimes more. But we can't help if we don't know.

I'll be honest: I don't like the word failure as I feel it has too strong of an emotion attached. I prefer to look at everything as an experience. However, this is one time that I am glad that I feel like I failed.

Life is a beautiful ride if we let it be so. It is our choice, even when we don't feel we have control. I can tell you that we most certainly do.

Life is full of every emotion we are programmed with, and we will feel all of them throughout our lives.

Each moment is a new one and one we create. If you want more information on how to create your life experiences intentionally, I have my resources listed on the *"About Me"* page.

Your Life is Your Flow and Always Your Choice.

And I am forever fortunately failed.

- M. LaRae, M. Sc.
Metaphysician/Intuitive/Best Selling Author/Reiki Master

Dear Friend,

You are loved. The Universe is within, and it is all love. You live in that. And you can access that at any time. Be free. Face it. Face your dilemma. The hero is inside. The superhero is inside you. You are the superhero. Lift yourself out of your dilemma. It is possible. Yes, you can. Face it first. Be all that you can be.

- Marvin Ginsberg

"What is that man doing in the attic? Oh my god, he is always at something!" I rolled my eyes to heaven. I was in the kitchen with my mam and my 16-month-old daughter. My dad had gone upstairs to use the bathroom, and my husband was still asleep in the next room. About 10 minutes later, my life would change forever and never be the same again. Who would have thought someone you love could take their own life in a house with three other people in it and succeed? My husband found my dad, and I will never forget the piercing screams, tumbling down the stairs, and that terrifying horror in his face and voice. He could hardly breathe, let alone speak. I knew something terrible had happened, so I tried to calm the situation and ask. He kept saying I can't tell you. Call the guards and keep the door closed while in tears, shaking his head. Then, there was even more crying. I held his face and told him everything was going to be okay. I calmly walked over to the drawer, where I got a pair of scissors and a large kitchen knife. *"Where are you going?"*

I am going to take him down. I am not leaving my father like this. My mam was hysterical at this point. I went in to get our neighbor and friend next door and asked her to come in and keep my mam and daughter in the kitchen and not let them come out. My husband rang emergency services. We walked up the stairs, and he told me not to look up! As I got closer, I turned my head to the right, and through the balusters at the top of the landing, there were my dad's little slippers and feet about one foot off the ground. I slowly started to move my eyes up until I could see everything.

My heart was broken, and I also felt numb. We both got my father down. I remember thinking what a hideous color of rope; it was orange. The ambulance was on the way and on the phone with us. I had to check for a pulse on his neck and wrist, but there was none. I had to try CPR, and I couldn't do it. I was 27 years old and had no first-aid training. I never thought in a million years that I would ever be in this position, nor did I want to be. I remained calm as tears rolled down my cheeks. I was definitely in shock and maybe adrenaline, too. When the guards arrived, they asked questions and searched the home, garden, shed, and attic for a letter or a note from my dad. I had to remind them that my dad couldn't read or write, so there would be no letter. That all sounds very long, but everything happened so fast. It was 11th December 2005; we buried him on the 17th, the week before Christmas.

I went straight back to work as if nothing had happened and studied, and I wouldn't take time off. I felt alright, or so I thought. Plus, as I did not live where my home place was, it was so easy not to tell anyone or talk about it. After a couple of weeks, while driving to work like any other day, these emotions and feelings came over me in waves. I could not control them! They hit me like a truck. Grief, loss, anger, guilt, shame, fear, panic, but mostly, I felt the most excruciating pain in my heart that I have ever felt. I could hardly breathe and see the road in front of me. I almost crashed my car with all these realizations hitting me at once. I pulled onto the side of the road, rang work, and could hardly speak words. I told them I would not be in and had to leave. I felt like I was broken in every way you could imagine. Mentally, physically, and emotionally.

For me, I felt so much pain that I actually thought I could die from this pain. It was there all of the time. Nights were awful; once the nightmares started, it was every night. Flashbacks, terror, seeing him every night in horrible circumstances over and over again. I would be afraid to sleep and then wake up exhausted. I had also realized I was pregnant and expecting our second child. I was now concerned with looking after myself and my daughter every day while experiencing this grief or process I was going through. Myself and my husband couldn't really talk about it as he was also struggling. I couldn't tell the doctors exactly what was happening as I thought they would take my daughter and see me as an unfit parent. I did not speak to family or friends as I did not want to look weak and certainly did not want to have them look at me with pity on their faces. No way. I was strong, and that was that. Plus, speaking about anything else that was going on in my head was a welcoming distraction, even if it was only for a little while. I felt trapped with my thoughts, which were now going from bad to worse, as were the nightmares.

Driving my car was so scary, and I had become so afraid of my own thoughts that my knuckles would be white from holding the steering wheel so tight to keep it straight. This constant battle going on in my head was exhausting. While pretending to the world that I was fine. *"Just crash the car, and all this pain will stop, and you will never have to feel like this again,"* these thoughts were getting louder every day. Sometimes, I had to shout NO really loud. I felt like I was totally out of control and disappearing. Then, I would look in the rearview mirror and see my baby girl in the back seat. I wondered if this would ever stop. I was so afraid and tired of it all. I didn't like going down the hall in my home as every time I would see my dad there from the attic, I couldn't look in the mirrors, and I hated it when there were doors left half open. I saw him everywhere now. The pain is growing and consuming me completely.

A few months passed, and I started to bleed a little, so I went to the doctor; he said to rest and keep my feet up for a few days and that it may stop. If not, there was nothing we could do. I would lose my baby. To be honest, I was numb and not feeling myself at all. I continued to bleed in the next few days, and I miscarried. I went to the hospital, and a scan confirmed it. I remained in for the night for a D and C procedure and was put in a ward with new mums and their babies. I remained calm, and it was devastating. I thought what a strange thing to do to put a mother who just lost her baby into a ward with newborns. The conversations were tough, as you can imagine. I then had more grief and more leaflets to read, this time about miscarriage. I shoved them in the drawer with all my other leaflets and booklets on suicide and grief. I then started to think that I was being punished because I couldn't save my dad. I should have saved him. I felt I was now a terrible daughter and an even worse mother. That I didn't deserve anything good or happiness. Guilt and shame were at the top of the list now! My feelings were starting to overwhelm me. I did not want to be here anymore; let's face it, the world would be so much better without me. I was worthless. I was no longer pregnant. I was in a terrible state on one particular day and finally got the courage to call a suicide line; it was the weekend I got put through to a recording that said they could not take my call and to call this other number. I was shocked and so angry in tears and thought that I must be so bad that even the people who helped didn't want to speak to me either. I wondered if they realized how much it took out of me to call in the first place. I was furious. I felt as though I was at the edge of a cliff and wanted to jump. I did not call the other number. I was so angry; this was ridiculous. Who is going to help me now? I went to my doctor and asked him if he would be able to help me improve my mood. I was trying to make it sound not that serious, and on the inside, I was capable of absolutely anything; it was frightening. I was given a prescription for antidepressants; I took them for two weeks only. The bad thoughts took me to a whole new level. Crying in the shower with music on was useful. Nobody knew!

Did I forget to mention I was also back in the workplace? I have to say, on the outside, I looked great and had a positive, annoying, optimistic personality, and work was a great distraction again. Anyone who was talking to me would never know unless I told them. Everything on the outside looked perfect, and everything on the inside was like an apocalypse on a catastrophic scale. Being alone was my most dangerous time, especially in the car. While at home, my little girl was always with me. She was and still is my world. Thoughts were getting out of control, so much so that writing a letter and leaving it for my husband was on my mind 24/7. It would be so easy to run a bath, cut myself, and drift off!! To wake up every day feeling pain and thoughts now was all-consuming, and fighting to get through the day was hard. I was so afraid for myself, and the last thing I wanted to do was leave my daughter. Myself and my husband were growing apart. My father had left me, and I refused to do the same to my daughter. So, to give up was not an option; I had to fight every day. Within the next six months, our marriage was broken. We still lived together but had no trust. My world was in total chaos, and I couldn't talk about it. I also didn't want to, as if I said everything out loud. I did not know if I would be able to survive. What the fuck am I going to do? I cannot live like this anymore. I am so emotionally tired. It was draining. I have to live for my daughter. That's what kept me here. I must live. I have to do better. I can do better.

"Awaking is not changing who you are, but discarding who you are not."
Deepak Chopra

It was now about 18 months after my dad had taken his own life. I kept seeing this book advertised everywhere and hearing about it on the radio: *"The Secret"* by Rhonda Byrne. I was in Eason Book Store one day, and there it was right in front of me. I had a quick glance over the first few pages, and as I read the first few lines, they resonated so much with me at that moment. It read, *"A year ago, my life had collapsed around me. I'd worked myself into exhaustion, my father died suddenly, and my relationships with my work colleagues and loved ones were in turmoil. Little did I know at the time, out of my greatest despair was to come the greatest gift."* well, if this isn't a sign, then I don't know what is. If this didn't give me hope, nothing would! I read a few more bits and pieces.

Bob Proctor, philosopher, author, and personal coach, *"The Secret gives you anything you want: happiness, health and wealth."*

John Assarf, an entrepreneur and money-making expert, said, *"We can have whatever it is that we choose. I don't care how big it is."*

It talked about the laws of the universe and that we all work with one infinite power. This Secret was about the law of attraction. I had never heard about this before. It was as if I had no choice but to buy that book. I was so excited to get stuck in. That was going to change my life. I didn't know how; I just knew that it would. I was going to read it, study it, and do what the book told me. I loved it from the moment I held it in my hand, and I couldn't put it down. I thought this was incredible. Your thoughts become things, and you can have anything you want. I quickly realized that I had a lot of work to do on my mindset, the thoughts I had, and how they made me feel emotionally and physically. That everything was connected.

I first learned that what you focus on and put your energy into grows. I was eating, breathing the Secret. I was becoming more aware every day of what I thought about and how it affected me on a daily basis. I became more aware of the words I spoke to myself and others. I started to use my imagination. I wondered why They did not teach us this in school. I discovered that working on myself was the only way I would feel better, act better, and have a happy life. It was my responsibility. I realized for the first time that I actually got to choose. I decide what thoughts I want to keep and what I want to eliminate.

That took discipline on my behalf and lots of persistence. I had to create new habits that would improve my life. I was determined to do whatever it took. I had a daughter to raise. Quitting was not one of my options. I learned about gratitude. I kept a journal, which I still do. It is such a massive part of recovery from any trauma. The Secret taught me so much about mindset, the law of attraction, and manifestation. That was the start of my personal development journey and my first book on the subject. I quickly learned how to control myself and manifest many things, including going on a lottery TV game show called Winning Streak. I won 32,800 euros. I bought lots more books and practiced meditation every day. *"The Power of Now"* by Eckhart Tuile teaches you how to stay in the present moment. If you are experiencing depression, thinking about the past, and experiencing anxiety, you are thinking and worried about the future. All we have is this moment right now. Whatever you are doing at this moment, be fully present and use all of your senses; this will keep you in the present. Life is a journey; we are here to experience everything. We experience life through our perception of our environment, family, school, friends, community, and religion. What we believe is based mainly on what we were told to believe and how we should and should not behave. What is expected and what is not by society. To conform to what we think will make everyone else happy.

I have been on this journey of personal development and healing for almost 17 years, and yes, there is still so much to learn, and I will never know it all. I went into mentorship studying *"Thinking into Results"* and completed *"Ignite"* with Kim Calvert. She is Bob Proctor's number-one consultant. It was an incredible experience. I have learned so much and met amazing people; some became lifelong friends. Here, I learned about decision-making, responsibility, paradigms, and the importance of scheduling to give myself more time. How to set goals and achieve them. To act as if until I become that person. How to improve your image.

Push myself out of my comfort zone and know everything always works for you. I know this will find the people who need to hear my story, and I want to tell you that there is no growth without challenges. No matter how hard they seem, you will get through them and learn so much about yourself, how strong you are, how brave you are, and how much you will fight for the life you want. I focused on my daughter, so find your purpose for living and concentrate only on that. Keep it at the front of everything else. You will succeed in overcoming whatever it is that you need to.

One of the affirmations I used a lot while in recovery *"I am whole, perfect, strong, powerful, loving, harmonious, and happy"*

I would focus on this affirmation when a bad thought entered my mind. It was on repeat all the time! You have to be consistent and persistent!! There are so many incredible books that have helped me. I continue to educate myself on a daily basis. To try my best to be better than I was the day before.

Books on my shelf that help me
"The Power of Your Subconscious Mind" by Dr.Joseph Murphy
"The Four Agreements" by Don Miguel Ruiz
"The Success Principles" by Jack Canfield
"Conversations With God" by Neale Donald Walsch

My checklist of stuff that actually works!!
Talk to a therapist (one whom you feel a genuine connection with)
Meditation
Breathwork
Gratitude journal: 10 things you are grateful for
Write a self-image script in the present tense
Keep a goal card to keep you focused
Observe your thoughts and ask yourself if they serve you
Replace negative thoughts with a positive idea (short affirmations are great).
Acknowledge how you feel and be gentle with yourself
Cold showers are great (if you are brave)
Vision boards are great fun
Check-in with yourself hourly. How was I feeling? What was I thinking about? Then, consciously choose to think about what you want.
Be positive, persistent, and patient.
Be consistent
Create new habits
Surround yourself with people who will encourage you and support you
Lots of self-care and self-love

I found that personal development saved my life, and I feel so blessed to be here and to share with you what has helped me. Please know that you are never alone.

The most important BELIEVE IN YOURSELF!!

PRACTICE DAILY and be RELENTLESS!!

Much Love,
Lisa X

- Lisa Powell

Dear Self,

I remember the day that death whispered to us in that silent song. I know how tempting it is to fall under its siren's song. How many times has it beckoned to us with the offer of peace and release from our pain and torments? It was never so tempting as this cold day you are experiencing now.

The ice is on everything. The trees look like they are covered in glass. I remember the crunch of it under our feet as we walked down the road to the bus stop. School is the only warm place in your life right now. You have to make it there. I remember the moment we stopped walking. The moment death's song whispered to us in silence. It talks to you about peace and release. The peace looks a lot like this icy day. It is a way to end the pain of neglect and cruelty. It is the path to let go of the deep hurt gouging at our soul from all the words spoken in hate and maliciousness. Words like 'slow,' 'witch bitch', 'demon spawn,' and 'stupid.'

It is whispering to you about the release of your physical pain, too. The pain in your chest with each breath you take can just go away. There will be no more struggle to have anything. Food will be nothing to you. Water will be nothing to you. That is what death sings to you in the silence. I remember it. It sings of nothingness.

The ice and quiet of the world around you is the image we have of death. Frozen. A stillness that coats everything.

Death whispers to you about just stopping there. Give into the cold that seeps into every cell of your body. Sit down and just stop breathing. It would not take long. Not in this frozen world. The elements will take you away before school is even over. You don't even own a coat. In your short sleeves, thin cotton shirt, and thin pants, you would not last long. Just sit down. Don't take another step. Just quit, and it will all be over soon.

Death is the option out of all the pain and struggle of life. That is what we believe at this moment. Trust me when I say it is. Death is the end of life. Trust me when I say don't stop now. Don't quit moving. You must keep moving. Death is the release you dream of. It is also the end of all choices. You have to know that winter always ends. Spring is not far away.

No matter how hard it is in this moment, the next moment, and the moment after that, there comes a moment that saves us. In the next breath, you will hear the branch crack and break from the frozen trees. It will snap away death's song. You will make it to school. There, a teacher will see how sick you are. She will inform someone. You will be sent to the hospital. Don't give in to the temptation of that siren's song.

You will find peace in living. Trust me. Life is a struggle that is brutal and messy. It is also beautiful. You and I have a son now. We have dogs. I know that is hard to believe! We do! We have dogs. People listen to our words. We help so many others now. You don't know this at this time. All you know is the numb pain that is every minute that you are existing. Trust me. Death will take away all our choices. There are so many for us to make. You feel there are none right now. There is a choice. Move forward and live. Don't give up. No matter what, that spring moment will come. You have to believe me.

You are not evil. You are not stupid. You are amazing. You will always be amazing. Death is an answer that ends all other options, my beautiful self. It is an answer that ends all choices. It is not peace. It is not being released. It is finality and blackness. The world has so many colors. Squirrels are so fun to watch! The taste of chocolate is a miracle you cannot give up! There are the yellow flowers in autumn that hold your attention for hours. You will lie under trees of green on the warm ground. There is the feeling of pride we have in our beautiful son when he becomes an amazing man. Take that next step. There is a beautiful world that will explode into spring for you soon. Don't quit. Don't give up.

That is the branch breaking. I don't know why it snaps us back to life. Maybe it was this letter reaching out from time and space. I know you walk to the bus stop. I know we get on that cold bus. I know we make it to school. I know the end of this story. At this time, you do not, though. It does not end happily ever after. It ends with adventure, excitement, joy, anger, pain, happiness, and the ups and downs of living a life worth living. Thank you for not giving up. Thank you for moving forward, no matter what. I love you, self. I always will.

Sincerely,
You

- Anonymous

MESSAGES OF HOPE

We collected some messages from those who have struggled with self-harm and suicide on:
"What help/advice can you offer someone who is going through a similar situation?"
Here were their unedited answers to messages of hope they wanted to share with you:

"Face it, go within. The hero is inside. It is YOU bathed in total Love."

"Time heals everything, that's the saying isn't it. No one ever tells you how much time it takes. They give you different ways to heal, ways that may have worked for someone else, and they expect it to help everyone the same way. The truth is everyone heals differently, and at different paces. I'm still healing, and I think I will be for a while. The way you choose to heal, the timeframe you heal in, may not look the same as someone else's healing journey, but that doesn't mean you're doing it wrong. Healing is meant to be for YOU. You get to set boundaries, you get to be selfish, you get to make the decisions, when it comes to your mental health. You don't have to apologize for your story or your journey. Past me never would've done this. It was years before I convinced myself to tell my friends and family. Even now, this is the

first time I'm sharing my past in such an open manner. I'm not saying that you must share your story, that's a choice you must make on your own. I am saying you need to own your story, your journey, your past. Don't let it control you. Don't let who you were then dictate who you are now. You deserve to heal, to grow, to learn, to fight for yourself. You matter more than you think or know. So, fight with all the strength you have, and when you feel like giving up, have the strength to ask for help. Be brave enough to understand that you are not alone. Have faith in the knowledge that you are capable of doing this. You don't always have to have it all together, but when you feel like you're falling apart, just know that there is someone who is willing to help stand up. 'Your mental health is everything – prioritize it. Make the time like your life depends on it, because it does.' ~ Mel Robbins"

"Take your medication, stay in therapy, discover a faith discipline(that can help you when you experience times that you don't believe in yourself and you can rely on your Higher Power), don't isolate, build a solid social network, get enough sleep, keep up your daily living skills, and reach out whenever you need to."

"If you have suicidal ideas, talk about it to a trusted!! family member or friend, or to a trained counselor. Also, always try to maintain yourself well regarding eating, sleep, etc.."

"Don't give up."

It is okay to not be okay. Reach out to those who can help and if you feel you cannot do that, find somewhere you feel safe enough to check out and get help (for me it is a local hospital I did my rehab in after my suicide attempt). Be brave enough to see the signs when they start to spiral again and make the decision to get help then instead of waiting. You are not alone, no matter how much you might feel you are. You are loved and you matter."

APPENDIX ON
END - OF - LIFE CHOICES

Includes 'Barbara's Choice' & Resources

A definition of terms:

Euthanasia: A doctor is allowed by law to end a person's life by a painless means, as long as the person and their family agree.

Assisted suicide: A doctor assists an individual in taking their own life if the person requests it.

VSED (voluntarily stopping eating & drinking): occurs when a mentally capable individual decides to control their own death by making a conscious decision to refuse foods and fluids of any kind, including artificial nutrition and/or hydration, in order to advance the time of their death. Supported by Compassion & Choices

The following states allow medical aid in dying: California, Colorado, Washington D.C, Hawai'i, New Jersey, Maine, New Mexico, Oregon, Montana, and Washington. Austria, Belgium, Canada, Luxembourg, The Netherlands, New

Zealand, Portugal, Spain, and Switzerland are the only countries internationally that allow medical aid for dying.

In certain life circumstances, an individual may feel that they are tired or that life is no longer worth living. People with terminal illnesses, chronic health conditions, and/or severe mental health problems, which "steal the minimal amount of joy," may feel that life is no longer worth living. VAD is legally accepted in only eleven states of The United States of America and nine countries worldwide. Many feel it is not up to the individual to decide when to die. In certain religions, such as Catholicism, assisted suicide is considered a sin. In Judaism, it is forbidden.

We thought it essential to include this section, not to condone suicide in any form, but to explore and expand our thinking around end-of-life care. My question to you is - what is life? Would you say "life" is being sustained by a machine so that vitals are maintained, but the person has no active part in their own life? I view living as including a certain autonomy over our life choices, including our deaths and end-of-life care.

I have always believed that we, as adult human beings, have autonomy over our lives. In the following story, Barbara's choice, I tell the story of my mother's decision to incorporate VSED (voluntarily stopping eating & drinking) into her end-of-life care. I was with her during this time, and we were able to consult with a doctor. The reason that this was not a legal issue is that I administered morphine for pain. The doctor prescribed it and consulted with us but did not dispense the medication. My mother chose a passive form of suicide, which entailed stopping eating and drinking (VSED). That did not involve any medication to assist her dying process, as she abstained from foods and liquids. Morphine (for pain) and Ativan (for anxiety) were the only medicines dispensed.

My mother always said she did not want to live life as a "vegetable." She always reminded us over the years about her DNR order (do not resuscitate.) Have you given any thought to how you envision your final days? Perhaps start a conversation with a loved one or a professional. It is essential to have all your wishes in writing, whether in a living will, DNR order, or advanced directives, including who you assign to be your healthcare proxy, to make decisions on your behalf should you become unable to do so.

Barbara's Choice

My mom passed over on Mother's Day. Call it a coincidence, but it would seem appropriate if you knew my mom. She decided to end her own life. It wasn't because of depression or suicidality, but because at 85 years old, she was tired. She felt she had lived a long and, for the most part, successful life.
My mom had birthed four children, had eight grandchildren, traveled the world, and married four times. Mom was the first person in her family to attend college. She was born in The Bronx, a single child of immigrant parents from Odessa. On

her train ride from Grand Concourse in The Bronx to Brooklyn College, she learned how to read *The New York Times*. Mom was a guidance counselor in the New York City parochial schools, then rose to the position of coordinator of the guidance program while simultaneously raising four children.

My mother lived hard and played hard. She gave her all to most things, including her death. During the 1950s, she desperately wanted children and was having complications getting pregnant. At a time when artificial insemination was not widely accepted, Mom did it twice. During later marriages, she was able to get pregnant and had two more children, including me!

Barbara continued to forge ahead in her brazen independence and utter disregard for the opinions of others. At 65, she took the law boards to gain entrance into law school. While she ended up not pursuing this option, it was yet another example of her strength of character and optimism. The world was there for her taking, and she went forth into the world, learning at every opportunity, even into her 80s.

Barbara ran a group called Death Cafe in her retirement community. She spoke openly about her thoughts on outliving a productive and satisfying life. Much to the chagrin of her fellow residents, Mom was often vocal about her feelings, popular or not. One of her beautiful qualities was her belief in helping those who were less fortunate. As a teen, I accompanied her to overnight women's homeless shelters to volunteer. As she often reminded me, upon returning home from the shelter, we would see our own home with such gratitude.

My mom loved having children but was not so fond of the early years; she found them boring and routine. Before returning home to her second job as a mother to the four of us and dog and wife to her husband, she would often sit in a coffee shop to decompress from the stresses of the work day.

My mom had told my brothers and me that she might decide to stop eating and drinking at some point in her life. In preparation for this juncture, she interviewed the retirement community director, where she lived in the northeast part of the United States. Barbara Taylor, who had been heavyset for most of her life after bearing children, was greeted with laughter in response to this. The director retorted, "*You* are going to stop eating?!" My mother was the epitome of determination; with 90% of her planets in Capricorn, as much as we wanted or tried to, there was no dissuading her.

My daughter, then eight years old, and I were traveling up to see my mom for her spring break in April. That is when I received that fateful email from Mom stating, "I know it won't be of great surprise to you, but I have decided to end my life." I received this email while sitting on the Dartmouth Coach about an hour away from our destination. My daughter was in the bathroom while I was in such shock and crying uncontrollably.

I tried to hide my grief, but my kid knew me too well. Ellie kept asking me what was wrong. I was not prepared to share or explain this to her; how do you explain that Grandma is checking out and will not be alive for much longer? I had to think fast and think through the grief quickly swelling up inside me. There were many physical ailments I could try to pin this decision on; Mom had recently broken a few ribs during a fall and was in a lot of pain, plus she had atrial fibrillation. Her asthma was severe, and it had become increasingly difficult for her to walk. She had visited her oral surgeon and was told she would need a total reconstruction of her jaw, which her cancer medication had eaten away; Barbara was a two-time cancer survivor and had been in remission for many years.

None of these seemed to be enough of a reason. None were life-threatening. But for now, I could not tell my daughter. In many ways, she was closer to her than most of us. I could not tell her that her grandma had decided to die of her own accord. I ended up telling her that it was a heart issue. In many ways, it was. As Ellie grew up, I shared Barbara's choice with her.

I was to arrive on Monday morning, May 4, 2015, where we would embark on this journey between life and death together. I would accompany Mom to the death's door and ensure she safely arrived before I took my leave. In Dr. Barbara Taylor fashion, she had begun the day before without me: her last meal on a flight back from her grandson's graduation in Michigan. Really, Mom? Plane food? I arrived with my family on Monday. They had come to say goodbye to her and return home. I would remain for the duration. Little did we know it would only take a week.

The first few days were very "normal." I remember looking for a book to read to help pass the time. When I perused my mom's nearly empty bookshelves and remarked that she might have left a few books for me to read, she said, "I told you last month to take what you wanted." It hadn't felt right to begin taking Mom's things while she was still very much alive. I learned my lesson.

I got a couple of Mom's favorite movies out of the library, one of which was *Cabaret*. Mom would drift off during the movie and come back around. By day two, she would drift off more often. I remember one morning, she insisted she should wake up early, and I reminded her that she could rest now. I removed her watch as we drifted into the timelessness that would be her last week on Earth. My youngest brother came at some point between Wednesday and Thursday, days three and four.

By Thursday, day four, Mom fell into a coma. I continued to administer morphine every few hours and more frequently as needed. I set an alarm on my phone for the night hours, lest she not feel the pain of dehydration. I recalled the night nursing of my two kids that blended with the bittersweet wakings of this particular time.

I wasn't clear how much time we had left, but I knew it was getting closer quickly. My friend Lois, a nurse practitioner, informed me that hearing was the last sense to go. She encouraged me to continue talking with my mom. I got into bed with her and held her hand. I said, "Mom, I'm sorry for anything I did that hurt you. Please forgive me. I forgive you for anything you did that hurt me, intentionally or unintentionally." She squeezed my hand in recognition of my words. That was one of the moments that will forever be branded in my mind. It was our last reciprocal communication in life.

My oldest brother, Peter, was on a business trip in Australia. He was always available to me when I had questions about anything and was particularly helpful about morphine dosages and overall support. We had agreed that I would be in touch by text regarding timing. That night, I texted him and suggested he return to Mom as the voyage was long, and we had no definitive sense of time. We did not know it at the time, but we only had two more days and a few hours left with Mom.

I would whisper in her ear that Peter was on his way; he was in Los Angeles getting a flight back to Boston. Robert, my middle brother, would pick him up at the Boston airport and head up to New Hampshire. By this time, it was late in the night on Saturday. Josh, my youngest brother, and I waited by

Mom's side for the others to arrive. It was after midnight when they did, on Sunday, Mother's Day. I moved to let Peter sit near Mom's head. Hours from death, she squeezed his hand to tell him that she knew he had arrived and that we were all there with her for our final earthly goodbye.

At about 1:30 a.m., Peter said, "These may be her final breaths." In fact, three deep breaths later, Mom's soul would be free of her earthly body. She lay on her deathbed with Peter on her right side, reading Kaddish, the Jewish prayer for the dead, and me on her left side, reading *The Tibetan Book of the Dead*. All four of her children were with her for her final breaths.

I consider myself a brave person, but I wasn't sure how I would get through this. Many of my friends were shocked and asked exactly how I did. I suppose part of me has inherited my mom's iron will; it was something that needed to be done, and I did it. I remember when Mom first told me I was quite upset, sad, and then angry. I felt she was shorting us. As the week went by, my anger transformed into gratitude, and I had a deeper understanding of the titanic nature of my mother's request. She had always been a person who liked to be in control. How awesome was it that she would hand over control of her life to me in this sacred trust? I was to be her end-of-life advocate, just as she had nurtured and advocated for me from conception. At one point, she said to me, "I was there for the beginning of your life. It seems only fitting that you should be here at the end of mine."

I've been asked how this experience has changed me. I learned more than ever how strong I was during this time. I was able to give my mother the ultimate gift of autonomy over her own life. My mother did not want to live a life without purpose. She would walk through the halls of her retirement community and point out others who had lapsed into a vegetative state or could not remember anything. She would say, "I don't want to end up like this," and would proceed to remind me about her DNR or her do not resuscitate order.

I have survived many difficult things in my life: I have lost both parents, terminated a pregnancy resulting from rape, been in emotionally and verbally abusive relationships, gotten a divorce, and turned my father away from my home because he was too intoxicated the last time I saw him before his death. Accompanying my mother to her afterlife was by far one of the hardest. It was painful losing her earthly self that had birthed me, nourished me with her milk, and raised me into the woman I am today. However, knowing that her final wish was to die with dignity and on her terms, I was able to overcome my personal pain to grant her this wish.

I was not able to work for some time. Because of the nature of my work as a psychotherapist, I couldn't "sort of" be there; I had to be fully present or not at all. I chose not at all. For a good year, I studied Western astrology. I watched every video Astrolada put out. That was one of the silver linings: in my grief, I learned a skill that gave me hope and is profoundly mystical and practical. I am now studying Vedic astrology, a far vaster and more ancient realm of astrology. I guess I have Mom to thank. Some days, I cried. My kids listened and comforted me. My son said, "We can be your parents." My daughter, only eight, and with me when my mom announced her intentions that April, always supported me.

Nothing will ever feel as hard; difficult conversations and situations pale in comparison to the final week I spent with my mom. I know I can say hard things and be honest about my feelings. Illness, physical and emotional, and death are some of the most challenging parts of life. Something about how my mom went about her end of life was more difficult because it was not natural; it was something she planned. As much as being a part of her plan helped me, it was not what I would have chosen. There were so many life experiences we had yet to experience together. She would never see my kids graduate, marry, or have their own kids. We had planned to take a river cruise in Ukraine, where her father was born. Mom said she needed a year to save for it. Unbeknownst to us, we would take a different journey together.

I remind myself of the Herculean task I completed with and for her. Some people say she was selfish, and maybe so. But the alternative was heartbreaking. It was heartbreaking for anyone, but particularly for someone like my mom, who was staunchly independent and driven. There was no compromise. It had to be her way. I respect and honor that this was the path she chose. I am moved that she invited me to be her partner on this final journey. I miss her every day and am comforted to know her soul is free, unencumbered by earthly limitations.

If this is a scenario you find yourself dealing with, I suggest getting support from someone who is non-judgmental and supportive of you and this process. I was lucky to have tremendous emotional support from family and friends. Remember that hearing is the last sense to go. Talk to your loved one. Tell them your last words, and ask for forgiveness. Forgive them. That will make your heart lighter. Relationships are never easy. Final words and forgiveness are vital as a means to grieve and process loss. I did not have this closure with my father, and it took years of hard work in therapy and spiritual practice to heal from that sudden loss. I would be happy to help you on this journey. Please reach out for a coaching or therapy session.

Lastly, remember what a gift this is to your loved one. While it was one of my hardest life tasks, accompanying my mom on her journey was a sacred partnership I will always treasure.

- Jen Taylor, LCSW

APPENDIX ON SUICIDE RESOURCES

**Includes Resources for
Suicide Help & Assessment**

List of Suicide Help & Hotlines[1]:
(United States and Worldwide)

United States:
Emergency: 911
Suicide Hotline: 988

Algeria:
Emergency: 34342 and 43
Suicide Hotline: 0021 3983 2000 58

Angola:
Emergency: 113

---

[1] List of Helplines and Hotline Numbers Retrieved from blog.opencounseling.com

Argentina:
Emergency: 911
Suicide Hotline: 135

Armenia:
Emergency: 911 and 112
Suicide Hotline: (2) 538194

Australia:
Emergency: 000
Suicide Hotline: 131114

Austria:
Emergency: 112
Telefonseelsorge 24/7 142
Rat auf Draht 24/7 147 (Youth)

Bahamas:
Emergency: 911
Suicide Hotline: (2) 322-2763

Bahrain:
Emergency: 999

Bangladesh:
Emergency: 999

Barbados:
Emergency: 911
Suicide Hotline Samaritan Barbados: (246) 4299999

Belgium:
Emergency: 112
Suicide Hotline Stichting Zelfmoordlijn: 1813

Bolivia:
Emergency: 911
Suicide Hotline: 3911270

Bosnia & Herzegovina:
Suicide Hotline: 080 05 03 05

Botswana:
Emergency: 911
Suicide Hotline: +2673911270

Brazil:
Emergency: 188

Bulgaria:
Emergency: 112
Suicide Hotline: 0035 9249 17 223

Burundi:
Emergency: 117

Burkina Faso:
Emergency: 17

Canada:
Emergency: 911
Suicide Hotline: 1 (822) 456 4566

Chad:
Emergency: 2251-1237

China:
Emergency: 110
Suicide Hotline: 800-810-1117

Columbia:
24/7 Helpline in Barranquilla: 1(00 57 5) 372 27 27
24/7 Hotline Bogota: (57-1 323 24 25

Congo:
Emergency: 117

Costa Rica:
Emergency: 911
Suicide Hotline: 506-253-5439

Croatia:
Emergency: 112

Cyprus:
Emergency: 112
Suicide Hotline: 8000 7773

Czech Republic:
Emergency: 112

Denmark:
Emergency: 112
Suicide Hotline: 4570201201

Dominican Republic:
Emergency: 911
Suicide Hotline: (809) 562-3500

Ecuador:
Emergency: 911

Egypt:
Emergency: 122
Suicide Hotline: 131114

El Salvador:
Emergency: 911
Suicide Hotline: 126

Equatorial Guinea:
Emergency: 114

Estonia:
Emergency:112
Suicide Hotline: 3726558088
In Russian: 3726555688

Ethiopia:
Emergency: 911

Finland:
Emergency: 112
Suicide Hotline: 010 195 202

France:
Emergency: 112
Suicide Hotline: 0145394000

Germany:
Emergency: 112
Suicide Hotline: 0800 111 0 111

Ghana:
Emergency: 999
Suicide Hotline: 2332 444 71279

Greece:
Emergency: 1018

Guatemala:
Emergency: 110
Suicide Hotline: 5392-5953

Guinea:
Emergency: 117

Guinea Bissau:
Emergency: 117

Guyana:
Emergency: 999
Suicide Hotline: 223-0001

Holland:
Suicide Hotline: 09000767

Hong Kong:
Emergency: 999
Suicide Hotline: 852 2382 0000

Hungary:
Emergency: 112
Suicide Hotline: 116123

India:
Emergency: 112
Suicide Hotline: 8888817666

Indonesia:
Emergency: 112
Suicide Hotline: 1-800-273-8255

Iran:
Emergency: 110
Suicide Hotline: 1480

Ireland:
Emergency: 116123
Suicide Hotline: +4408457909090

Israel:
Emergency: 100
Suicide Hotline: 1201

Italy:
Emergency: 112
Suicide Hotline: 800860022

Jamaica:
Suicide Hotline: 1-888-429-KARE (5273)

Japan:
Emergency: 110
Suicide Hotline: 810352869090

Jordan:
Emergency: 911
Suicide Hotline: 110

Kenya:
Emergency: 999
Suicide Hotline: 722178177

Kuwait:
Emergency: 112
Suicide Hotline: 94069304

Latvia:
Emergency: 113
Suicide Hotline: 371 67222922

Lebanon:
Suicide Hotline: 1564

Liberia:
Emergency: 911
Suicide Hotline: 6534308

Luxembourg:
Emergency: 112
Suicide Hotline: 352 45 45 45

Madagascar:
Emergency: 117

Malaysia:
Emergency: 999
Suicide Hotline: (06) 2842500

Mali:
Emergency: 8000-1115

Malta:
Suicide Hotline: 179

Mauritius:
Emergency: 112
Suicide Hotline: +230 800 93 93

Mexico:
Emergency: 911
Suicide Hotline: 5255102550

Netherlands:
Emergency: 112
Suicide Hotline: 900 0113

New Zealand:
Emergency: 111
Suicide Hotline: 1737

Niger:
Emergency: 112

Nigeria:
Suicide Hotline: 234 8092106493

Norway:
Emergency: 112
Suicide Hotline: +4781533300

Pakistan:
Emergency: 115

Peru:
Emergency: 911
Suicide Hotline: 381-3695

Philippines:
Emergency: 911
Suicide Hotline: 028969191

Poland:
Emergency: 112
Suicide Hotline: 5270000

Portugal:
Emergency: 112
Suicide Hotline: 21 854 07 40
And 8 96 898 21 50

Qatar:
Emergency: 999

Romania:
Emergency: 112
Suicide Hotline: 0800 801200

Russia:
Emergency: 112
Suicide Hotline: 0078202577577

Saint Vincent and the Grenadines:
Suicide Hotline: 9784 456 1044

São Tomé and Príncipe:
Suicide Hotline: (239) 222-12-22 ext. 123

Saudi Arabia:
Emergency: 112

Serbia:
Suicide Hotline: (+381) 21-6623-393

Senegal:
Emergency: 17

Singapore:
Emergency: 999
Suicide Hotline: 1 800 2214444

Spain:
Emergency: 112
Suicide Hotline: 914590050

South Africa:
Emergency: 10111
Suicide Hotline: 0514445691

South Korea:
Emergency: 112
Suicide Hotline: (02) 7158600

Sri Lanka:
Suicide Hotline: 011 057 2222662

Sudan:
Suicide Hotline: (249) 11-555-253

Sweden:
Emergency: 112
Suicide Hotline: 46317112400

Switzerland:
Emergency: 112
Suicide Hotline: 143

Tanzania:
Emergency: 112

Thailand:
Suicide Hotline: (02) 713-6793

Tonga:
Suicide Hotline: 23000

Trinidad and Tobago:
Suicide Hotline: (868) 645 2800

Tunisia:
Emergency: 197

Turkey:
Emergency: 112

Uganda:
Emergency: 112
Suicide Hotline: 0800 21 21 21

United Arab Emirates:
Suicide Hotline: 800 46342

United Kingdom:
Emergency: 112
Suicide Hotline: 0800 689 5652

United States:
Emergency: 911
Suicide Hotline: 988

Zambia:
Emergency: 999
Suicide Hotline: +260960264040

Zimbabwe:
Emergency: 999
Suicide Hotline: 080 12 333 333

CONDUCT A SUICIDE INQUIRY[2]

A. Ideation

Frequency, Intensity and Duration

- Have you had thoughts of hurting yourself or others?
- Have you thought about ending your life?

Now, in the Past, and at its Worst

- During the last 48 hours, past month, and worst ever: How much? How intense? Lasting for how long?

B. Plan

Timing, Location, Lethality, Availability/Means

- When you think about killing yourself or ending your life, what do you imagine?
- When? Where? How would you do it? In what way?

---

[2] Retrieved from Minnesota Department of Health at: https://www.health.state.mn.us/people/syringe/suicide.pdf

Preparatory Acts

- What steps have you taken to prepare to kill yourself, if any?

C. Behavior

Past attempts, aborted attempts, rehearsals

- Have you ever thought about or tried to kill yourself in the past?
- Have you ever taken any actions to rehearse or practice ending your life (e.g., tying noose, loading gun, measuring substance)?

Non-suicidal self-injurious behavior

- Are you having paranoid thoughts? Hallucinations?
- Have you done anything to hurt yourself (e.g., cutting, burning or mutilation)?

D. Intent

Extent to which they expect to carry out the plan and believe the plan to be lethal versus harmful.

- What do you think will happen?

- What things put you at risk of ending your life or killing yourself (reasons to die)?
- What things prevent you from killing yourself and keep you safe (reasons to live)?

Explore ambivalence between reasons to die and reasons to live. Pay attention to how they describe the outcome.

- "I'm dead, it's over." indicates a higher risk of suicide death.
- "I think I'd end up in the hospital." indicates a moderate risk of suicide death.
- "I don't want to die; I want my suffering to end." indicates a lower risk of suicide death.

E. Notes

- When working with **youth**, collect information from a parent, guardian or service provider on the youth's suicidal thoughts, plans, behaviors, and changes in mood, behavior or disposition.
- If the person has thoughts or plans to **harm someone else**, conduct a homicide inquiry using the same questions (replace "hurt or kill yourself" with "hurt or kill someone else").

DETERMINE RISK LEVEL[3]

The risk level is determined with the previous three steps:
1. Risk Factors
2. Protective Factors
3. Suicide Inquiry

Death by Suicide Risk Level

Risk Level	Risk Factors	Protective Factors	Suicide Inquiry	Intervention*
High	Multiple risk factors	Protective factors are not present or not relevant at this time	Potentially lethal suicide attempt or persistent ideation with strong intent or suicide rehearsal	Hospital admission generally indicated, suicide precautions (e.g., observation, means reduction)

---

[3] Retrieved from Minnesota Department of Health at: https://www.health.state.mn.us/people/syringe/suicide.pdf

Moderate	Multiple risk factors	Few protective factors	Suicidal ideation with a plan, but not intent or behavior	Hospital admission may be necessary, develop crisis plan and suicide precautions, give emergency/crisis numbers
Low	Few and/or modifiable risk factors	Strong protective factors	Thoughts of death with no plan, intent or behavior	Outpatient referral, symptom reduction, give emergency/crisis numbers

Take every suicide attempt seriously!

People often think a person is not really suicidal.

It's better to be safe, even if they will be angry with you for taking action to keep them alive.

ABOUT THE AUTHOR

Jen Taylor, LCSW
#1 International Bestselling Author

Jen Taylor, LCSW is a New York-based spiritual psychotherapist with 23+ years of experience. Jen specializes in womens' empowerment, domestic violence, teens, and LGBTQIA+ individuals. Jen incorporates spirituality and astrology into her sessions to create a truly unique blend of guidance.

Jen was born and raised in New York City and lived there from preschool through high school. Instead of attending her prom, Jen went to boot camp for the Navy and received accreditation as a U.S. Naval photographer. Jen then received her Bachelor's in Arts from Haverford College in Pennsylvania and studied abroad in Florence, Italy. She spent her early

20s in the advertising office of Italian *Vogue* and went on to attend social work school at Fordham University's Graduate school of social services. In 1999, Jen received her Master's in social work while pregnant with her first child, Giancarlo. Jen worked in various outpatient mental health clinics in New York City, and in 2007 had her second child, Elisabetta.

Jen Taylor, LCSW is the editor for Girl on Fire Magazine's "Wine Down with Jen," where she uses her 20+ years of experience as a New York-based spiritual psychotherapist to bring you cozy couch conversations you would have with your best friend over a glass of wine after work.

When not writing for the magazine or seeing clients, Jen enjoys traveling, photography, spending time with her kids, and a good cup of coffee.

Jen is a multiple #1 International bestselling author in a collaboration series and currently working on releasing the rest of this series as her very first solo books over the next year.

To connect with Jen, she can be reached at jentaylorscw@gmail.com